I0467020

AMERICA
THE
BEAUTIFUL

DAVID COPE

© David Cope 2024.

All Rights Reserved.
Published 2024.

COAST TO COAST AND BEYOND

THE MAINE COAST, MAINE

THE NORTH WOODS

SQUAM LAKES, NEW HAMPSHIRE

STOWE, VERMONT

THE GREAT BEACH,
MASSACHUSETTS

CONCORD, MASSACHUSETTS

NEWPORT, RHODE ISLAND

BLOCK ISLAND, RHODE ISLAND

MYSTIC, CONNECTICUT

THE ADIRONDACKS, NEW YORK

WEST POINT, NEW YORK

NIAGARA FALLS, NEW YORK

THE CLOISTERS, NEW YORK

MAIN BEACH, NEW YORK

THE PINE BARRENS, NEW JERSEY

CAPE MAY, NEW JERSEY

LONGWOOD GARDENS, PENNSYLVANIA

INDEPENDENCE MALL, PENNSYLVANIA

GETTYSBURG, PENNSYLVANIA

CHESAPEAKE BAY, MARYLAND

WASHINGTON BAY, D.C.

THE NEW RIVER, WEST VIRGINIA

COLONIAL WILLIAMSBURG, VIRGINIA

FALLINGWATER,
PENNSYLVANIA

INDEPENDENCE MALL,
PENNSYLVANIA

GETTYSBURG, PENNSYLVANIA

WINTERTHUR, DELAWARE

CHESAPEAKE BAY, MARYLAND

THE NEW RIVER, WEST VIRGINIA

WILLIAMSBURG, VIRGINIA

SHENANDOAH. PARK

OUTER BANKS, NORTH CAROLINA

CHARLESTON,

SOUTH CAROLINA

GOLDEN ISLES, GEORGIA

SAVANNAH, GEORGIA

SANIBEL ISLAND, FLORIDA

EVERGLADES, FLORIDA

FLORIDA, KEYS

NATCHEZ, MISSISSIPPI

RYMAN AUDITORIUM, TENNESSEE

MAMMOTH CAVE

OTTAWA, OHIO

GREAT SERPENT MOUND

MACKINAC ISLAND, MICHIGAN

AMISH COUNTRY, INDIANA

DOOR PENINSULA, WISCONSIN

HAMMOCK OM A WINDY DAY

RAIN ON A PORCH

COTTAGES IN PROVINCETOWN

HOUSES AS A STORM ROLES IN

VOYAGEURS, MINNESOTA

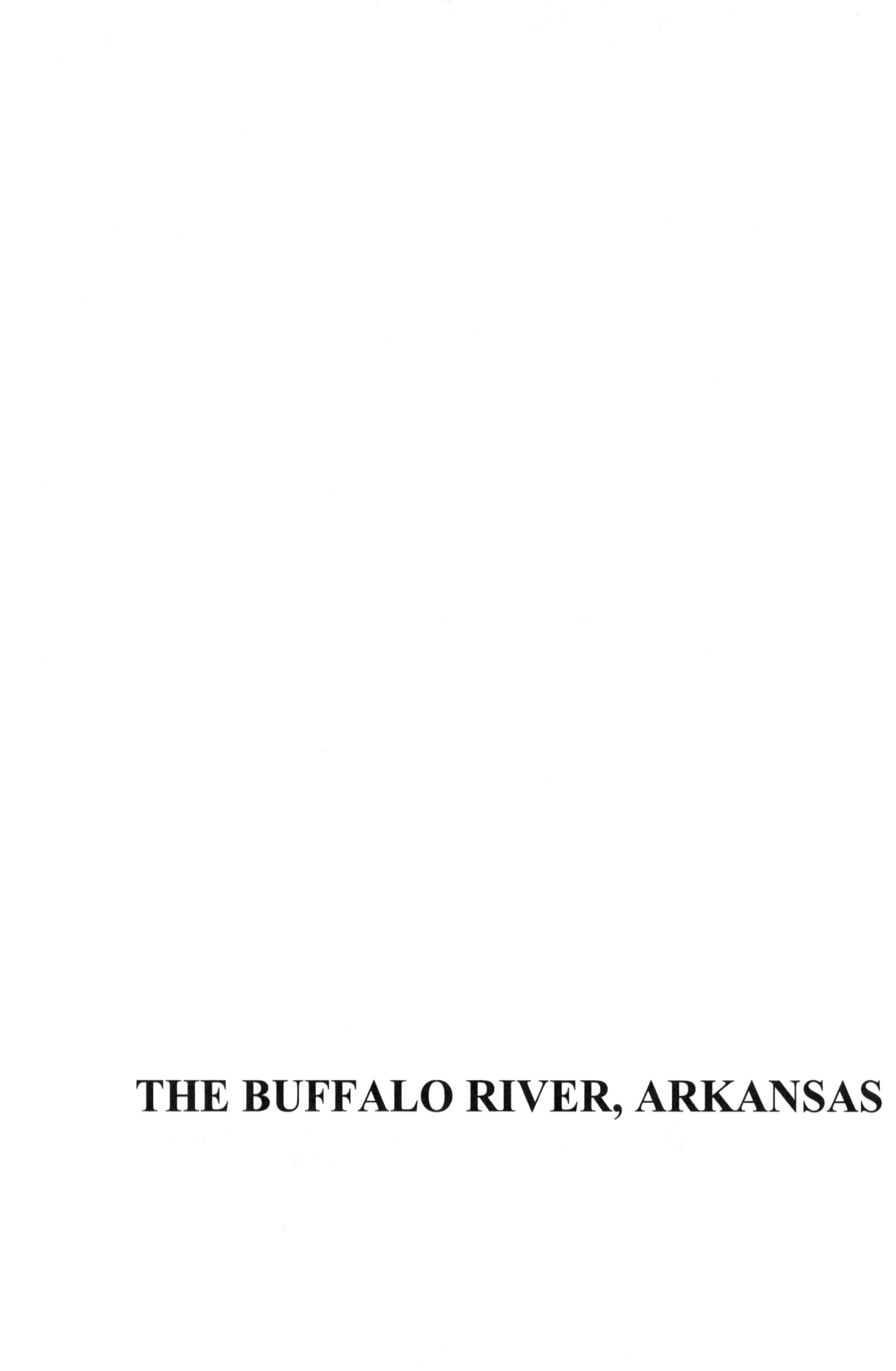

THE BUFFALO RIVER, ARKANSAS

THE ALAMO, TEXAS

BEAVERS BEND, OKLAHOMA

CHIMNEY ROCK, NEBRASKA

FLINT HILLS, KANSAS

GLACIER NATIONAL PARK, MONTANA

BEARTOOTH HIGHWAY, MONTANA AND WYOMING

YELLOWSTONE, WYOMING, MONTANA, AND IDAHO

TETONS, WYOMING

THE GREAT DIVIDE, COLORADO

TELLURIDE

SANTA FE, NEW MEXICO

WHITE SANDS, NEW MEXICO

THE ANASAZI RUINS

CARLSBAD CAVERNS, NEW MEXCO

RED ROCK COUNTRY, ARIZONA

GRAND CANYON, ARIZ0NA

MONUMENT VALLEY, UTAH

CANYONLANDS, UTAH

BRYCE CANYON

ARCHES

ZION PARK, UTAH

LAKE TAHOE, NEVADA

SAN JUAN ISLANDS, WASHINGTON

MOUNT RAINIER

MULTNOMAH FALLS, OREGON

UMPQUA FOREST, OREGON

CASCADE LAKES, OREGON

REDWOODS, CALIFORNIA

SAN FRANCISCO

YOSEMITE

BIG SUR

DEATH VALLEY

JOSHUA TREE

SAN JUAN CAPISTRANO

YOSEMITE

CALIFORNIA BLACK OAKS IN THE ANWAHNEE MEADOW

GLACIER POINT

BRIDALVEIL FALL

EAGLE PEAK IN WINTER

ARTIC OUT THERE

GATES OF THE ARTIC

GLACIER BAY

KENAI FJORDS

KATMAI, ALASKA

DENALI

BIG ISLANDS VOLCANOES, HAWAII

ST. JOHN, VIRGIN ISLANDS

MAUI

COAST TO COAST AND BEYOND

THE MAINE COAST, MAINE

THE NORTH WOODS

SQUAM LAKES, NEW HAMPSHIRE

STOWE, VERMONT

THE GREAT BEACH,
MASSACHUSETTS

CONCORD, MASSACHUSETTS

NEWPORT, RHODE ISLAND

BLOCK ISLAND, RHODE ISLAND

MYSTIC, CONNECTICUT

THE ADIRONDACKS, NEW YORK

WEST POINT, NEW YORK

NIAGARA FALLS, NEW YORK

THE CLOISTERS, NEW YORK

MAIN BEACH, NEW YORK

THE PINE BARRENS, NEW JERSEY

CAPE MAY, NEW JERSEY

LONGWOOD GARDENS, PENNSYLVANIA

INDEPENDENCE MALL, PENNSYLVANIA

GETTYSBURG, PENNSYLVANIA

CHESAPEAKE BAY, MARYLAND

WASHINGTON BAY, D.C.

THE NEW RIVER, WEST VIRGINIA

COLONIAL WILLIAMSBURG,
VIRGINIA

FALLINGWATER, PENNSYLVANIA

INDEPENDENCE MALL,
PENNSYLVANIA

GETTYSBURG, PENNSYLVANIA

WINTERTHUR, DELAWARE

CHESAPEAKE BAY, MARYLAND

THE NEW RIVER, WEST VIRGINIA

WILLIAMSBURG, VIRGINIA

SHENANDOAH. PARK

OUTER BANKS, NORTH CAROLINA

CHARLESTON,

SOUTH CAROLINA

GOLDEN ISLES, GEORGIA

SAVANNAH, GEORGIA

SANIBEL ISLAND, FLORIDA

EVERGLADES, FLORIDA

FLORIDA, KEYS

NATCHEZ, MISSISSIPPI

RYMAN AUDITORIUM, TENNESSEE

MAMMOTH CAVE

OTTAWA, OHIO

GREAT SERPENT MOUND

MACKINAC ISLAND, MICHIGAN

AMISH COUNTRY, INDIANA

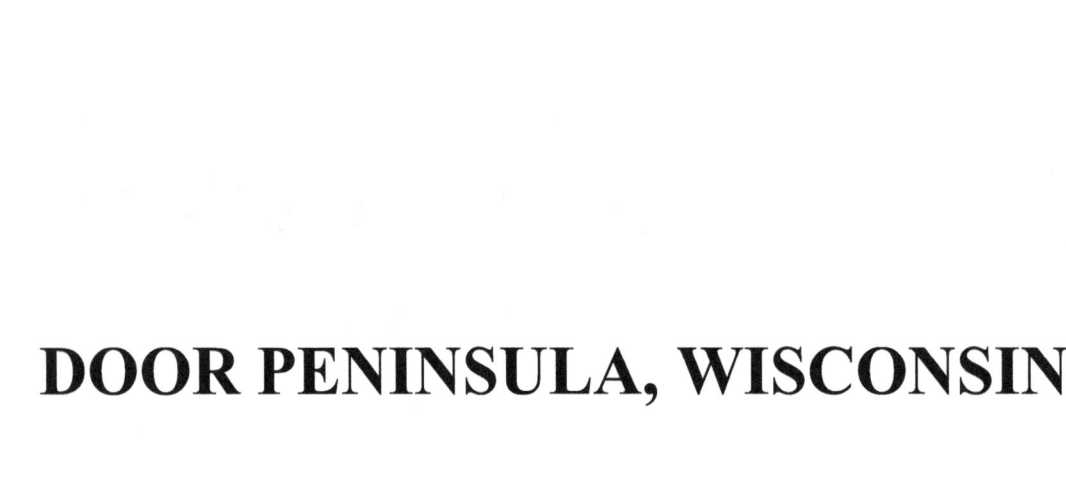

DOOR PENINSULA, WISCONSIN

HAMMOCK OM A WINDY DAY

RAIN ON A PORCH

COTTAGES IN PROVINCETOWN

HOUSES AS A STORM ROLES IN

VOYAGEURS, MINNESOTA

THE BUFFALO RIVER, ARKANSAS

THE ALAMO, TEXAS

BEAVERS BEND, OKLAHOMA

CHIMNEY ROCK, NEBRASKA

FLINT HILLS, KANSAS

GLACIER NATIONAL PARK, MONTANA

BEARTOOTH HIGHWAY, MONTANA AND WYOMING

YELLOWSTONE, WYOMING, MONTANA, AND IDAHO

TETONS, WYOMING

THE GREAT DIVIDE, COLORADO

TELLURIDE

SANTA FE, NEW MEXICO

WHITE SANDS, NEW MEXICO

THE ANASAZI RUINS

CARLSBAD CAVERNS, NEW MEXCO

RED ROCK COUNTRY, ARIZ0NA

GRAND CANYON, ARIZ0NA

MONUMENT VALLEY, UTAH

CANYONLANDS, UTAH

BRYCE CANYON

ARCHES

ZION PARK, UTAH

LAKE TAHOE, NEVADA

SAN JUAN ISLANDS, WASHINGTON

MOUNT RAINIER

MULTNOMAH FALLS, OREGON

UMPQUA FOREST, OREGON

CASCADE LAKES, OREGON

REDWOODS, CALIFORNIA

YOSEMITE

BIG SUR

DEATH VALLEY

JOSHUA TREE

SAN JUAN CAPISTRANO

YOSEMITE

CALIFORNIA BLACK OAKS IN
THE ANWAHNEE MEADOW

GLACIER POINT

BRIDALVEIL FALL

EAGLE PEAK IN WINTER

ARTIC OUT THERE

GATES OF THE ARTIC

GLACIER BAY

KENAI FJORDS

COAST TO COAST AND BEYOND

THE MAINE COAST, MAINE

THE NORTH WOODS

SQUAM LAKES, NEW HAMPSHIRE

STOWE, VERMONT

THE GREAT BEACH,
MASSACHUSETTS

CONCORD, MASSACHUSETTS

NEWPORT, RHODE ISLAND

BLOCK ISLAND, RHODE ISLAND

MYSTIC, CONNECTICUT

THE ADIRONDACKS, NEW YORK

WEST POINT, NEW YORK

NIAGARA FALLS, NEW YORK

THE CLOISTERS, NEW YORK

MAIN BEACH, NEW YORK

THE PINE BARRENS, NEW JERSEY

CAPE MAY, NEW JERSEY

LONGWOOD GARDENS, PENNSYLVANIA

INDEPENDENCE MALL, PENNSYLVANIA

GETTYSBURG, PENNSYLVANIA

CHESAPEAKE BAY, MARYLAND

WASHINGTON BAY, D.C.

THE NEW RIVER, WEST VIRGINIA

COLONIAL WILLIAMSBURG,
VIRGINIA

FALLINGWATER, PENNSYLVANIA

INDEPENDENCE MALL, PENNSYLVANIA

GETTYSBURG, PENNSYLVANIA

WINTERTHUR, DELAWARE

CHESAPEAKE BAY, MARYLAND

THE NEW RIVER, WEST VIRGINIA

WILLIAMSBURG, VIRGINIA

SHENANDOAH. PARK

OUTER BANKS, NORTH CAROLINA

CHARLESTON,

SOUTH CAROLINA

GOLDEN ISLES, GEORGIA

SAVANNAH, GEORGIA

SANIBEL ISLAND, FLORIDA

EVERGLADES, FLORIDA

FLORIDA, KEYS

NATCHEZ, MISSISSIPPI

RYMAN AUDITORIUM, TENNESSEE

MAMMOTH CAVE

OTTAWA, OHIO

GREAT SERPENT MOUND

MACKINAC ISLAND, MICHIGAN

AMISH COUNTRY, INDIANA

DOOR PENINSULA, WISCONSIN

HAMMOCK OM A WINDY DAY

RAIN ON A PORCH

COTTAGES IN PROVINCETOWN

HOUSES AS A STORM ROLES IN

VOYAGEURS, MINNESOTA

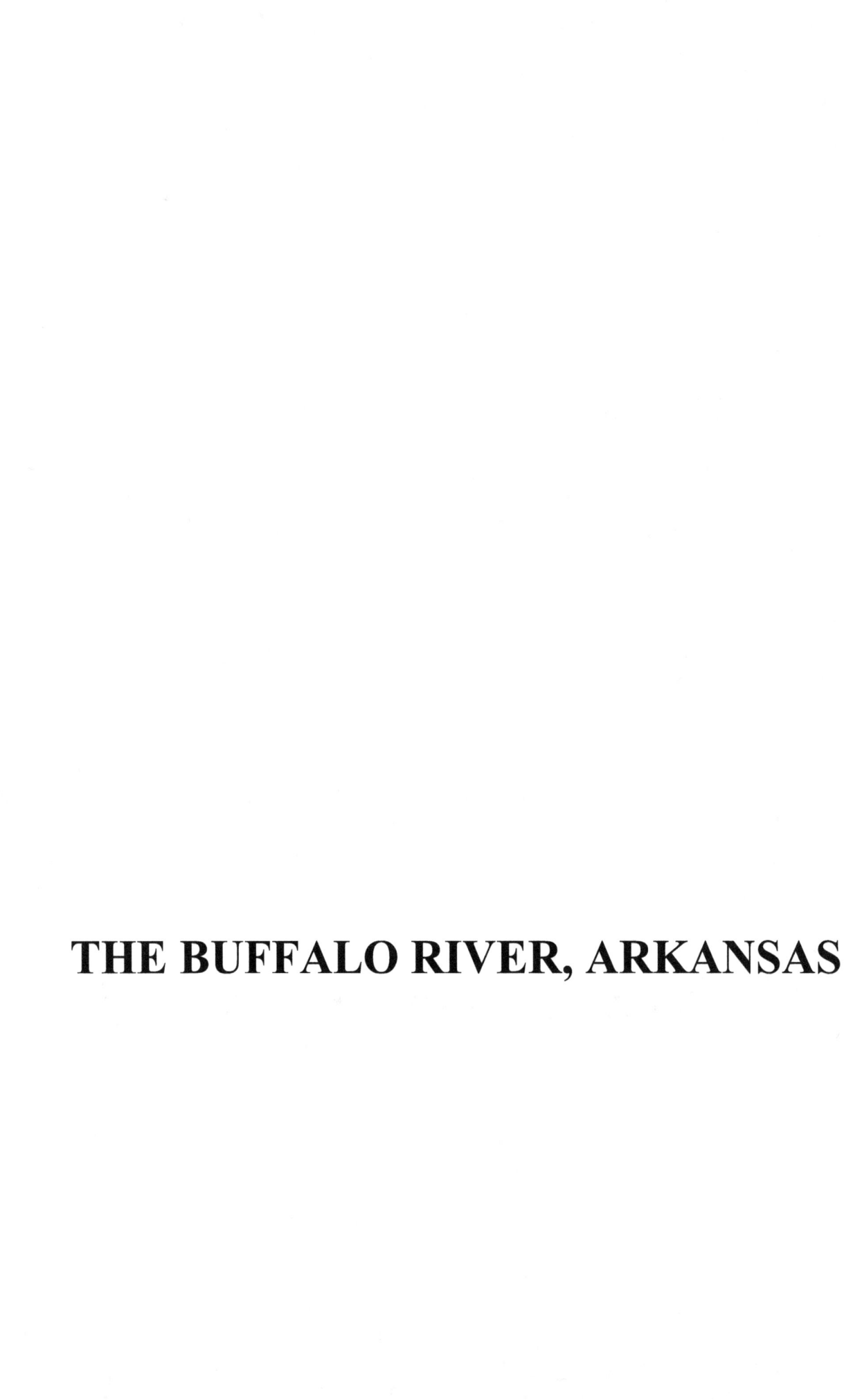

THE BUFFALO RIVER, ARKANSAS

THE ALAMO, TEXAS

BEAVERS BEND, OKLAHOMA

CHIMNEY ROCK, NEBRASKA

FLINT HILLS, KANSAS

GLACIER NATIONAL PARK, MONTANA

BEARTOOTH HIGHWAY, MONTANA AND WYOMING

YELLOWSTONE, WYOMING, MONTANA, AND IDAHO

TETONS, WYOMING

THE GREAT DIVIDE, COLORADO

TELLURIDE

SANTA FE, NEW MEXICO

WHITE SANDS, NEW MEXICO

THE ANASAZI RUINS

CARLSBAD CAVERNS, NEW MEXCO

RED ROCK COUNTRY, ARIZONA

GRAND CANYON, ARIZONA

MONUMENT VALLEY, UTAH

CANYONLANDS, UTAH

BRYCE CANYON

ARCHES

ZION PARK, UTAH

LAKE TAHOE, NEVADA

SAN JUAN ISLANDS, WASHINGTON

MOUNT RAINIER

MULTNOMAH FALLS, OREGON

CASCADE LAKES, OREGON

REDWOODS, CALIFORNIA

SAN FRANCISCO

YOSEMITE

BIG SUR

DEATH VALLEY

JOSHUA TREE

SAN JUAN CAPISTRANO

YOSEMITE

CALIFORNIA BLACK OAKS IN THE ANWAHNEE MEADOW

GLACIER POINT

BRIDALVEIL FALL

EAGLE PEAK IN WINTER

ARTIC OUT THERE

GATES OF THE ARTIC

GLACIER BAY

KENAI FJORDS

www.ingramcontent.com/pod-product-compliance
Lightning Source LLC
Chambersburg PA
CBHW082232220526
45479CB00005B/1207